ANATOMY OF A WINERY

THE ART OF WINE AT INNISKILLIN

DONALD J.P. ZIRALDO

FOREWORD BY
HUGH JOHNSON

INTRODUCTION BY
KARL KAISER AND DONALD ZIRALDO

DESIGNED AND ILLUSTRATED BY
SAM TURTON

KEY PORTER BOOKS

Dedicated to my Mom, Irma, and Dad, Fiorello.

My father died in 1964. I was 14 years old. In 1971, at my graduation from the University of Guelph, my mother presented me with my father's ring. The ring is solid gold from the McIntyre Mine in Timmins, Ontario, where he worked underground for 23 years. In 1974, three years later, I opened the winery. I have never removed the ring which I wear to this day. As if by destiny, the ring depicts clusters of grapes, vines and tendrils.

All author royalties from the sale of this book will be donated to the Canadian Cancer Society.

Technical Support: David Sheppard, Assistant Winemaker, Inniskillin Wines Inc.
Project Support: Deborah Pratt, Director of Public Relations, Inniskillin Wines Inc.

Photography:
Kevin Argue, pages 31, 43
Cork Quality Council, Napa, California, page 26(top R&L)
Cosmo Condina, page 41
Michael Foster, page 39
Dieter Hessel, pages 5, 13(L), 44, 45, 46
The Horticultural Research Station of Ontario, page 19(L)
Nigel Marson, page 10
James O'Mara, front cover, pages 7, 8, 11, 12, 14, 15, 16, 19,(R), 23, 27, 37, 38, 40, 47, 48
Lisio Plozner, Piero Pittaro, L'Uva e it Vino, pages 20, 21
Albert Scapillati, page 42(R)
Mark Shapiro, page 42(L)
Al Tone, Dofasco Inc., Hamilton, page 22
Tonnellerie Demptos, Bordeaux, France, page 25(B-L)
Wine Council of Ontario, page 13(R)

Canadian Cataloguing in Publication Data

Main entry under title:
Anatomy of a Winery

Includes index.
ISBN 1–55013–646-1

1. Inniskillin Wines Inc. 2. Wine and winemaking – Ontario – Niagara-on-the-Lake. 2. Wineries – Ontario – Niagara-on-the-Lake, Inniskillin Wines Inc.

TP559.C3A5 1995 663'.2'00971338 C95-930377-4

Key Porter Books Limited
70 The Esplanade
Toronto, Ontario
Canada M5E 1R2

Graphic assembly by Commercial Photo Copy Ltd., St. Catharines
Printed and bound in Canada by Arthurs-Jones Lithographing Ltd. (Leland Verner)

95 96 97 98 99 5 4 3 2 1

FOREWORD

Each of the world's classic wine regions has a distinctive identity of place. It can be as obvious as the Médoc, a long tongue of gravel and sand lapped by the Atlantic on one side and a broad river estuary on the other, or as subtle as the Côte d'Or, which on first sight seems interchangeable with a score of other hillsides in eastern France. However, when you get to know them well, their *terroir*, the sum of climate, soil and terrain that stamps their personality, becomes almost tangible; their style of wine its somehow inevitable product.

The vineyards of the Niagara Peninsula come into the "obvious" category. How could any territory be more clearly defined by nature than this lake-locked, escarpment-sheltered stretch of country? Its success as a fruit garden has long been well established. But until the 1970s it waited for its discoverers to realize it as wine country; the modern Canadian equivalent of the eager monks who created Burgundy (but with poverty, chastity and obedience optional).

Then suddenly it happened. Old fears and prejudices about the kinds of vines that could survive in Canada were tossed aside. The formidable knowhow that has been accumulating in new wine districts round the world provided answers to problems that had seemed insuperable. The 1980s saw Ontario take its place at the high table of the world's cool-climate wine regions. The 1990s are seeing it finesse its style, identify its most privileged sites and build its reputation beyond regional interest into the mainstream of the world's acknowledged fine wines.

Nobody will deny that in all this the Inniskillin winery has been the ice-breaker. Yet the creative dedication of Donald Ziraldo reaches far beyond his own winery. As Chairman of the Vintners Quality Alliance he is shaping the ambitions of Canada towards truly distinctive estate wines; the only route to international respect and trust.

And by the imaginative educational weapon of Inniskillin's self-guided winery tour he is teaching the new generation of Canadians to understand and appreciate the wines their country can make. This book is the logical, portable extension of the self-guided tour. It compresses, graphically and ingeniously, all the essentials of wine-knowledge into an evening's study.

I salute Donald Ziraldo, his partner, Karl Kaiser, and the staff at Inniskillin for another initiative that will demystify wine and bring it more friends. And I salute that ever-growing band of friends of wine and life.

HUGH JOHNSON
Author, **World Atlas of Wine, Pocket Encyclopedia of Wine** & others; host of T.V. series **Vintage: A History of Wine.**

"It was those Cistercians who started it all. They tasted the soil. They found the medium for expressing what they had discovered about the land they were working. And of course, they created a masterpiece for all time, one of the great masterpieces of the western world . . . the Cote d'Or.

Well, there are new masterpieces in the making, and I visited one this morning by helicopter. The other side of the lake. The Niagara Region. Nothing can be more thrilling than finding, being shown, a new wine region where these possibilities are being taken seriously."

Hugh Johnson; *excerpt from speech presented October 14, 1994, Granite Club, Toronto.*

INTRODUCTION

The Inniskillin winery exists because we believe that the making of wine is an art and that the experience of tasting good wine is one of life's highest pleasures.

Like all art forms, winemaking is deeply connected to the mastery of inspiration and creativity. Every grape variety is unique and is affected differently by the soil of each vineyard and the weather of every season. A winemaker's knowledge and intuition lead him through a labyrinth of choices, from grape variety and style of fermentation to oak variety and barrel aging. At every tasting each wine unveils something unique. Capturing the essential characteristics of each wine at their moment of perfection is the art of winemaking. It is what we take pride in at Inniskillin.

The idea for this book grew out of the popularity of the self-guided tour on-site at the Inniskillin winery. The tour itself was developed in 1992 when the building of our new Barrel Aging Cellar provided us with the opportunity to incorporate a self-guided tour into the rest of our construction. The overwhelming success of Inniskillin was drawing more and more visitors to the winery, and as these numbers grew, we needed to develop a means to provide more information about winemaking and Inniskillin than we could provide verbally.

We had discovered the concept of a self-guided tour at Sterling Vineyards in California's Napa Valley. We drew on this inspiration to devise our own tour, cutting viewing windows into the old and new buildings, so we could provide comfortable sightlines to all the viewable aspects of the winery and vineyards. Commentary, illustrations and photography set up at each viewing station explain the process of winemaking step-by-step.

The response to this tour has been phenomenal and many Inniskillin visitors have asked to have the information they experienced on the tour. In answer to these many requests and because we feel there is a real need for more information on our wine-growing region, we decided to write this book. Since the original idea, it has grown and developed into an educational tool to provide additional knowledge about cool-climate viticulture.

Turn the pages and you will be taken on the journey of wine. You will experience the climate, soil and geography that are unique to the Niagara Peninsula. You will discover just what it is like to grow grapes and make wine in a cool climate region and we will tell you about the Vintners Quality Alliance (VQA) and why it is important to winemakers like us. You will also learn about grape varieties and the virtues of cork- and barrel making – knowledge and skills shared by quality winemakers the world over.

We have focused, in this book, on cool climate viticulture. Therefore, we did not include a chapter on our Napa Valley venture where we, Inniskillin Napa Vineyards, are producing wines under the *Terra* label. We did include, however, another Canadian wine region, the Okanagan Valley, where we have entered into a partnership with the Inkameep Indian Band (Okanaquen tribe) to produce quality wines from one of Canada's other cool climate viticulture wine regions.

We are very proud of our many achievements at Inniskillin, such as our being awarded the coveted Grand Prix D'Honneur at Vinexpo in Bordeaux, France for our '89 Icewine.

As well we are very proud to share in the success and evolution of Niagara as one of the rising stars in the quiet revolution of New World wines. We thank you sincerely for the support and enthusiasm which has inspired us to achieve the successes thus afforded Inniskillin and the opportunity to create this book in celebration of the twentieth-year anniversary of our first vintage.

1974-1994.

ENJOY!

DONALD J.P. ZIRALDO
CO-FOUNDER

KARL KAISER
CO-FOUNDER

COOL CLIMATE VITICULTURE

Canada's Niagara Peninsula is located on the 43rd latitude, the same as northern California and more southerly than Burgundy!

The Niagara Peninsula is considered a cool climate viticulture region, as are Burgundy, Germany, Oregon and New Zealand. These regions are ideally suited for the growing of Chardonnay, Pinot Noir and Riesling. Wines from cooler climates are characteristically higher in acids and highly aromatic. These high acids result in wines, particularly white wines, with longer natural aging potential. Winemakers believe that cool climates produce lighter, fruitier wines whereas hotter regions produce less fruity, heavier wines.

One of the most famous wines produced in cool climate viticulture areas is Icewine (see pages 42-43). Icewine can be grown only in cool climate conditions and owes much of its greatness to the very high level of acidity in the wine. This acidity is necessary to sustain the great equilibrium between it and the tremendous concentration of sugar in the grapes and results in a beautifully balanced wine which has great finish on the palate.

The most important factor in Icewine production is low temperature during harvesting which increases the extract, fullness and aroma in the wine. The resulting high acidity (inherent in cool viticultural areas) is necessary to obtain the typical character of Icewines and is even more important than the sugar level of the grapes at harvest. Icewine is a high-risk wine, as yields are very low – often as little as 5 percent. The risk is even higher in Germany, where cold shocks are less regular.

Wine was grown in the cool climate viticulture regions of Burgundy and Germany as early as the first century. The first vineyards were established by the Romans, although it is believed that the Gauls had domesticated some wild vines for winemaking long before the Romans arrived. It is also thought that the Pinot Noir grape is an indigenous variety of Burgundy. The resistance to winter frost is a major characteristic of the grape. Quality Pinot Noir is best achieved under cool climate conditions. In warmer climates Pinot Noir loses its elegance and finesse. The slow maturing process seems to be a prerequisite for the manufacture of delicate aromas and freshness. Microclimatic differences influence the behaviour of Pinot Noir and the broad variation that can be found from vintage to vintage is an expression of that sensitivity. A good example of this is Pinot Noir in California where it best expresses these characteristics in the cooler Carneros region of Napa and Sonoma.

Chardonnay, on the other hand, is much more adaptable across a wide range of climatic conditions and can exhibit vastly different personalities. In warm climates such as Australia it tends to exhibit ripe, dense fruit flavours such as pineapple and mango paired with low acidity. Chardonnays from cool climates are characterized by their delicacy, finesse and firm acidity with subtle flavours of apple and grapefruit.

In general, cooler continental climates such as the Niagara Peninsula are subject to greater extremes – that is, hotter summers and cooler winters – than those of the warmer regions of Europe and California, resulting in considerable variability between seasons and vintages. Vintage charts from cool climate regions such as Burgundy show much more variability than do most vintage charts from hot climates such as Italy and Australia.

Cold winter temperatures are a significant limiting factor in viticulture. Winter injury can be quite common and if the temperature falls below -20° C, bud damage can occur. In North America, commercial viticulture is confined to southern regions such as California or water-moderated regions such as Long Island and Niagara. Continental viticultural areas are not only exposed to lower mid-winter temperatures, but are also subject to greater fluctuations in temperature. This results in a greater temperature range and subsequently more variable vintages.

Fortunately, Lake Ontario, a large, deep mass of water, has a major influence on the climate in the Niagara region. The lake absorbs and stores vast amounts of heat which it releases whenever the surrounding air and land are cooler than the lake. This continuous airflow over the surface of the land moderates winter temperatures and also reduces the risk of spring frost.

Another major criterion for cool climate definition is the rapid cooling of night temperatures during the crucial ripening months of September and October.

Northern latitudes, generally associated with cool climate viticulture, have shorter growing seasons. As a result, the rate at which grapes accumulate sugar and lose acid is slower than in more southern regions.

Latitude is also important as an indicator of climatic suitability. Latitude and altitude affect the amount and length of sunlight during the day and the relative coolness of night-time temperatures. In cool climate viticultural areas, solar deficiency produces high levels of odour-active

compounds because of slow fruit maturation. Odour-active compounds are detected by the nose and are recognized as familiar smells of grape (primary) aromas. An example of these aromatic esters and aldehydes would be terpinol in Gewürztraminer which produces a "spicy" odour.

There are several ways to measure the wine-growing potential of a region. The most common is growing degree days. They are measured as the sum of the monthly mean temperatures over 10° C, below which there is little, if any, physiological activity in the vines, from April 1st to October 31st. In terms of growing degree days, cool climate viticulture areas are mostly regions that are below 1426 growing degree days.

The following chart shows the median growing degree days in the major cool climate viticulture regions.

Growing degree days measured in Celsius:	
Geisenheim, Germany	1050
Epernay, France	1050
Hawk's Bay, New Zealand	1200
Roseburg, Oregon	1250
Geneva, Switzerland	1250
Beaune, France (Burgundy)	1315
Niagara, Canada	1426
Yakima, Washington	1426
Napa, California	1450
Healsburg, Sonoma, California	1755

The total amount of heat in growing degree days above 10°C, necessary for Riesling, Chardonnay and Pinot Noir varieties, should be between 1050 and 1450. If this is not attained the wines in most vintages will have to be "chaptalized" to maximize the wine's full potential of aroma, bouquet and balance.

The hours of sunshine and the temperature in a region play an important role in the growth potential of the vine. These two influences are interrelated but should not be confused. In cooler climates, temperature rather than sunshine becomes the limiting factor in determining the potential for growth. In warmer climates, temperatures are already adequate and it is the number of sunshine hours that will ultimately govern maturity.

As a perennial plant, grapevines have developed mechanisms to ensure survival during seasons of unfavourable weather. But to ensure long-term consistent production and to maintain the required quality of fruit in cooler climates, man becomes part of the survival mechanism through proper vineyard management.

There are many factors that are important in the ability to manage for cold endurance. The grower must understand the nature of vine maturation, dormancy, canopy management, training systems, rootstocks, water and soil management, nutrient requirements and clonal selection.

Clones are selected from a large population of grapevines. They exhibit superior characteristics and have two functions: to achieve specific and unique quality and to eliminate viruses. Clonal selection has played a large role in the development of cultivars specific to cool climate growing conditions. It enables the grower to select definite characteristics which, though not always immediately evident, may have a significant impact on the quality of the finished wine.

Besides the climate, a wine region's soil structure greatly determines the heat retention and water-holding capacity of the soil. This greatly influences the vine's performance and so the soil's structure is considered to be of even greater importance than its chemical composition. Climate may be the determining factor in deciding where to plant grapes and which grape varieties to plant. But the *terroir* will continue to be debated as the great contributor to the art of wine.

Top left: *Vineyard site on south shore of Lake Ontario.*

ANATOMY OF A WINERY

In *Webster's Ninth New Collegiate Dictionary,* the description of the word "anatomy" reads: "anatomy/Gk *anatome,* fr. *anatemnein* to dissect,: a separating or dividing into parts for detailed examination or analysis."

I chose the title *Anatomy Of A Winery* to reflect the self-guided tour. The twenty stations ("stations of the vine") of our on-site tour separate into parts the various aspects of grape growing and winemaking for a more detailed examination or analysis. The book follows both the vinification path and the path that our visitors take as they walk through the winery.

Anatomy also implies an "opening up," to look inside at how things work. Both the tour and the book are designed to do just that – open up the doors and walls to let you walk inside the world of wine.

It is amazing that, out of all the agricultural and industrial applications, no other single entity is more visited than a winery. This is because winemaking is more than an agricultural and industrial application of technology. It is an art form.

Below: *Station 11.* **PRESSING**

SELF GUIDED TOUR

Station Titles

1. **HISTORY OF INNISKILLIN**
2. **THE CLIMATE**
3. **SOIL AND GEOGRAPHY**
4. **VINTNERS QUALITY ALLIANCE – VQA**
5. **VITICULTURE**
6. **GRAPE VARIETIES**
7. **HARVESTING**
8. **COOPERAGE • The Art of Barrel Making**
9. **HISTORY OF THE CORK**
10. **DE-STEMMING/CRUSHING**
11. **PRESSING**
12. **FERMENTATION**
13. **RED WINES**
14. **WHITE WINES**
15. **TANK CELLAR**
16. **BARREL AGING • The Influence of Oak in Wine**
17. **BOTTLING LINE**
18. **BRAE BURN VINEYARD**
19. **ICEWINE**
20. **FRANK LLOYD WRIGHT**

WINE BOUTIQUE

HISTORY OF INNISKILLIN

On July 31, 1975, Inniskillin Wines incorporated and its founders Karl J. Kaiser and myself, Donald J.P. Ziraldo, were granted the first winery licence in Ontario, Canada, since 1929.

Established in Niagara-on-the-Lake and taking its name from the early history of the area, Inniskillin was founded upon and dedicated to the principle of producing and bottling outstanding wines from select wine grapes grown in the Niagara Peninsula, one of Canada's foremost wine-growing regions.

Before 1974, I had received my degree in agriculture from the University of Guelph and I was operating the family nursery specializing in fruit trees and grapevines. Karl, a native of Austria, had moved to Canada after meeting and marrying his Canadian wife, Sylvia. He had a degree in chemistry from Brock University and had begun experimenting with home winemaking.

One fateful day, Karl bought some French hybrid grapevines from me at the nursery and, some time afterward, we shared a bottle of Karl's very good wine. After a lot of dreaming and talking, we decided to apply for a wine licence. None had been issued since 1929.

But General George Kitching, Chairman, Liquor Control Board of Ontario, shared our vision of "a premium estate winery producing varietal wines from grapes grown in the Niagara Peninsula," and with his assistance, Inniskillin was born.

The first Inniskillin winery was housed in an old packing shed at the family nursery, two kilometres from our current location.

The name Inniskillin is Irish and is derived from the famous Irish regiment, the Inniskilling Fusiliers. Colonel Cooper, a member of this regiment, served in North America in the War of 1812. On completion of his military service, he was granted crown land which he named the Inniskillin Farm.

We were on our way.

As we grew we needed more space. And in 1978 we relocated to our present site, The Brae Burn Estate.

In building the new winery at Brae Burn we wanted to combine our experiences with those of both the Old and New World wine regions to create an estate winery that would harmonize architecturally with the natural and historic surroundings. The winery was designed by Raphaele Belvedere, a local architect, to allow our technological needs to blend with the historic environment of our site. It is adjacent to the

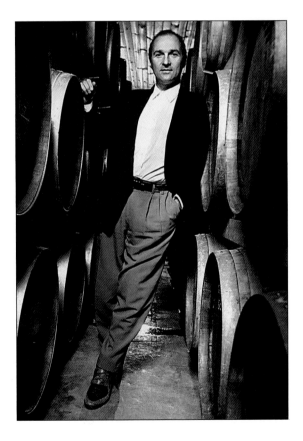

Donald J.P. Ziraldo

Karl J. Kaiser

existing Inniskillin vineyards, planted in 1974 by myself, and now known as the Seeger vineyard. The result, we believe, is a fine marriage of purpose, function and aesthetics.

The Brae Burn Barn

The historic Brae Burn Barn, constructed in the mid-1920s, houses the winery boutique, visitor centre and art gallery. The main floor consists of the retail wine boutique and tour centre, while the upper level loft, maintained in its original open-beamed structure, features the art gallery.

The barn and several others in the area were constructed in a similar style and are thought by many to be designed by the famed architect Frank Lloyd Wright, who designed the Larkin Building in Buffalo, New York.

Architects have admired the functional simplicity, integrity and craftsmanship of the barn. The word "barn" was originally created from the old English words *bere*, meaning barley and *ern* meaning a place for the laying up of any sort of grain, hay or straw. At Inniskillin we have adapted the meaning of barn as the laying down of fine wines.

Right: *The Brae Burn Barn and Wine Boutique.*

THE CLIMATE

As we discussed earlier, Niagara is considered a cool climate viticultural region, as are Burgundy, Germany, Oregon and New Zealand. These regions are ideally suited for the growing of Chardonnay, Pinot Noir and Riesling. Wines from cooler climates are characteristically higher in acids and highly aromatic. These acids result in wines that have longer natural aging potential. Malo-lactic fermentation, a natural microbial process, is used to reduce total acidity and add balance and finesse to the wines.

The Niagara Peninsula is located on the 43rd latitude, placing it in the same latitude as Northern California and more southerly than Burgundy which is on the 47th latitude, as illustrated below. With an average annual heat summation of 1426 growing degree days C (see page 6) the Niagara Peninsula falls into the category of cool climate.

Climatically, the Niagara Region is similar in many respects to Burgundy. Both are far from maritime influence and are affected by a continental climate. The annual rainfall of both is approximately 700 to 800mm and each can experience unpredictable September and October

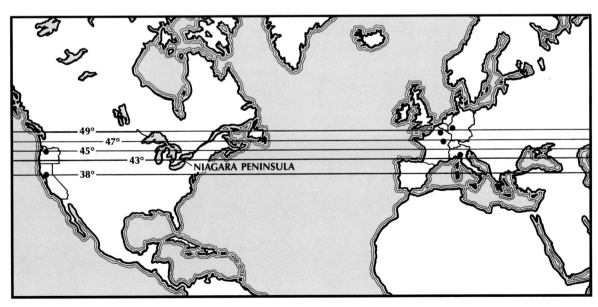

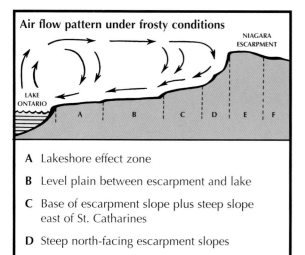

C. GRAPE CLIMATIC ZONES IN NIAGARA

Air flow pattern under frosty conditions

NIAGARA ESCARPMENT

LAKE ONTARIO

A B C D E F

A Lakeshore effect zone

B Level plain between escarpment and lake

C Base of escarpment slope plus steep slope east of St. Catharines

D Steep north-facing escarpment slopes

E Slopes above the escarpment

F Flat and rolling land south of the escarpment

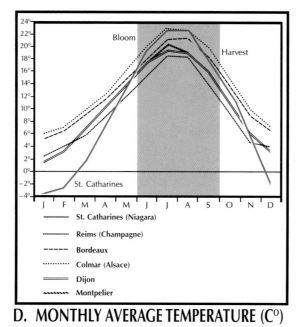

D. MONTHLY AVERAGE TEMPERATURE (C°)

Bloom

Harvest

St. Catharines

J F M A M J J A S O N D

—— St. Catharines (Niagara)

········· Reims (Champagne)

– – – Bordeaux

· · · · Colmar (Alsace)

═══ Dijon

∿∿∿ Montpelier

rains. The flowering in both regions generally occurs from about the 10th to the 18th of June, and although Burgundy experiences slightly more frost-free days than Niagara, we enjoy longer periods of daylight during July.

Burgundy and Niagara both enjoy long periods of daylight during the growing season.

The moderating effect of Lake Ontario is illustrated lower left (see Chart C). Together with the Niagara Escarpment (see photo top left), the lake creates a unique microclimate that allows for the growing of *Vitis vinifera*.

The region can be further subdivided into even smaller climatic zones as we have illustrated in Chart C.

If one uses a comparison based upon growing degree days (the summation of all degrees accumulated over 10°C during the potential growing season from April 1st to October 31st), the Niagara Peninsula compares favourably with some of the finest cool grape-growing areas, such as Burgundy or Region 1 in California (as defined by University of California, Davis, Climate Regions).

The most critical aspect of the growth cycle, as shown in Chart D, is that growth between bloom (June 10–18) and harvest (October–November) has approximately the same ripening period as other wine regions throughout the world, 100–112 days.

You will note that in Niagara this critical period is warmer than regions such as Alsace and Champagne. The graph in Chart D also illustrates that the cold winter temperatures in Niagara, which allow for the production of Icewine in December and January, generally will not affect the vines because they are in their dormant state.

SOIL AND GEOGRAPHY

Soil is a very critical element in viticulture. What follows is a description of the physiology and geology of the Niagara Peninsula, both of which ultimately affect the growing of grapes.

The Niagara Peninsula (see Chart A) is a distinct geological region situated in Southern Ontario, at 43°N in latitude. It is bound on the north by Lake Ontario, on the south by the shores of Lake Erie, and on the east by the Niagara River.

The backbone of the peninsula is the Niagara Escarpment, a *cuesta* (ridge) 30 to 50 metres high (see Chart B). This escarpment extends along the entire Niagara Peninsula and influences the soil and creates microclimates. North of the escarpment is a flat plain, the result of deposits (see Chart C) of lacustrine clays, sands and gravel whose original source was the bottom of the old Lake Iroquois. Lake Iroquois was a single lake that existed before the last Ice Age which caused the formation of the existing five Great Lakes. In some places the soil is modified by river valley alluvium, mostly sand and gravel. It is only in this area below the escarpment, and on the first bench, where the confluence of the escarpment and the lake favour the growing of premium grapes.

The types of rock found in the bedrock of the escarpment are siliceous sandstones, ferruginous sandstones, limestones and dolomites of Devonian age. Since the escarpment was at one time the shoreline of Lake Iroquois, the deposited soil is composed of many different types (clay, clay-loam, loam, sand, etc.) and changes frequently. The soils are generally deep and obtain a considerable quantity of mineral material from the different types of bedrock. All these rock types contribute material to the soils and ultimately influence the nutrition of the vineyards.

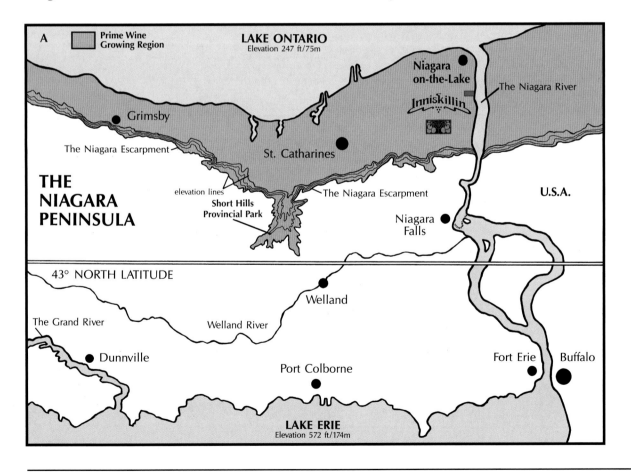

Below: *Niagara River as it flows north into Lake Ontario with Canada's Niagara Peninsula on the left. The United States appears on the right side of the river.*

B. ANATOMY OF THE NIAGARA ESCARPMENT

The influence of mineral deposits on Wine Region soils.

Note photograph bottom right

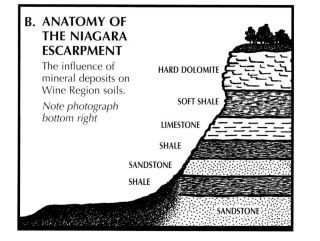

HARD DOLOMITE

SOFT SHALE

LIMESTONE

SHALE

SANDSTONE

SHALE

SANDSTONE

C. SOIL TYPES IN THE NIAGARA WINE-GROWING REGION
Cross-section of the Niagara Peninsula

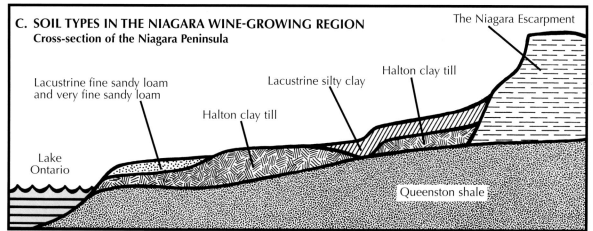

The Niagara Escarpment

Lacustrine fine sandy loam and very fine sandy loam

Lacustrine silty clay

Halton clay till

Halton clay till

Lake Ontario

Queenston shale

Below: *Queenston-Lewiston Bridge crossing the Niagara River at the Escarpment. See photo page 13.*

Bottom Right: *Face of the Niagara Escarpment with exposed bedrock.*

VINTNERS QUALITY ALLIANCE – VQA

The Vintners Quality Alliance – VQA – is an Appellation of Origin system by which consumers can identify wines of Ontario based on the origin of the grapes from which they are produced.

With the VQA system, Canada joins other leading wine-producing countries in developing a body of regulations and setting high standards for its finest wines. In 1935, for example, France introduced its *Appellation d'Origine Contrôlée* system that remains in place today. Italy introduced its *Denominazione d'Origine Controlata* designation in 1963. Germany's *Qualitatswein mit Predicat* system was finalized in 1971, and the US system in 1978.

In Ontario the VQA officially started in 1988. The Ontario VQA then requested that British Columbia undertake a similar system, which it did in 1990. Each region maintains several unique rules and regulations that are specific to it, just as Burgundy and Bordeaux do. All wine-growing regions in France function under the French Appellation of Origin system, governed by the *Institute National Des Appellations D'Origine* (INAO).

Experience has shown that certain vineyard areas, because of their favoured soils, exposure and microclimate, produce the best wines year after year. By designating the appellations of origin on the label, vintners provide the consumer with information about the origin of the grapes, particularly the *terroir* in which they are grown. As in the centuries-old wine regions of Burgundy and Chianti, refinements to the existing regulations within the VQA are continually being made.

There are two distinct wine-growing regions in Canada - the provinces of Ontario and British Columbia.

The VQA recognizes within Ontario three Designated Viticultural Areas (DVA): Niagara Peninsula, Pelee Island and Lake Erie North Shore. In British Columbia, the VQA recognizes four DVA: the Okanagan Valley, the Similkameen Valley, the Fraser Valley and Vancouver Island.

The VQA in Ontario is an independent alliance, with representatives from Ontario's wineries, grape growers, the Liquor Control Board of Ontario, and academic, hospitality and

DESIGNATED VITICULTURAL AREAS

Niagara Peninsula
Pelee Island
Lake Erie North Shore

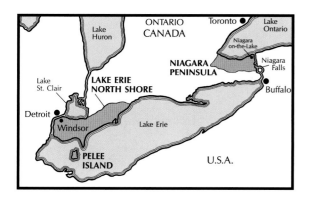

research institutions forming its Board of Directors.

A stringent code of regulations governs the right of vintners to use these highly specific geographic designations on their labels. Only *Vitis vinifera* varieties such as Chardonnay, Pinot Noir and Riesling can be used. The wine must be produced from 100 percent Ontario-grown grapes. For varietals, 85 percent of the wine must be made from the variety named on the label and must exhibit the predominant character of that variety. If a vintner wishes to designate the vineyard from which the wine was made, the site must be within a recognized viticultural area and 100 percent of the grapes must come from that vineyard. Wines described as estate bottled must be made from 100 percent grapes owned or controlled by the winery in a viticultural area. Minimum sugar levels have been set for vineyard

HOW TO READ AN INNISKILLIN WINE LABEL

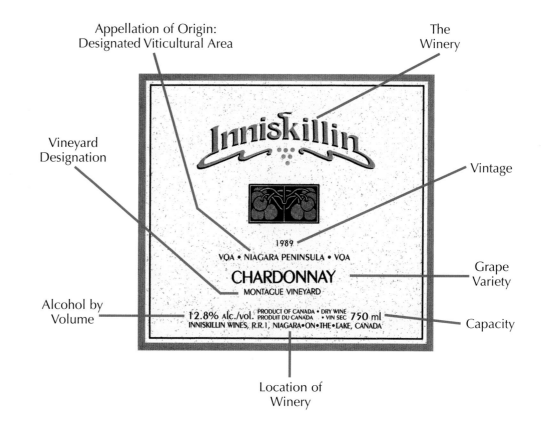

designated and estate-bottled wines, as well as dessert and Icewine.

Wines are evaluated by an independent panel of experts. Only those wines which meet or exceed the production and appellation standards are awarded VQA status and are entitled to display the VQA medallion. The gold VQA medallion is awarded only to those wines that perform exceptionally as judged by the VQA tasting panel.

VITICULTURE

"Our experience is that fine wines can only be made from excellent grapes. We are committed to growing and using only the finest quality grapes from our own vineyards and from a selected group of dedicated growers throughout the Niagara Peninsula who share our philosophy."

. . . Karl Kaiser

Inniskillin produces wines from the classic European grape species – *Vitis vinifera*. Several wines are also produced from French hybrid grape varieties. All grape varieties belong to the genus *Vitis*, meaning vine.

Grape Species

Vitis vinifera (*Vitis*-vine, *vinifera* - wine bearing)

The classic European species of vines whose origins date back to the Bible are known to originate from the region of Transcaucasia on the eastern shores of the Black Sea. Examples are Chardonnay, Pinot Noir, Riesling, Pinot Grigio and Cabernet Franc.

Hybrids

The original objective of crossing North American vines (*Vitis riparia*) with European vines (*Vitis vinifera*) was to develop a plant with a built-in resistance to the disease phylloxera but with European-tasting grapes. These French hybrids, often called direct producers (*producteurs directs*) since they are generally not grafted, initially formed the basis for the new generation of winegrowers in Ontario in the early 1970s, because of their hardiness, disease resistance and higher yields. Examples are Marechal Foch, Vidal and Seyval Blanc.

*Veraison

The point during the grape maturation process at which, simultaneously, the unripe grapes begin to change colour and their sugar content begins to increase.

○Pruning

A function of balancing the vine plant with the amount of fruit the vine must ripen. The grower's art is to assist the vine in optimizing that balance.

Opposite page left: *Grape blossoms in June.*
Opposite page right: *Fully mature cluster of grape berries in September.*

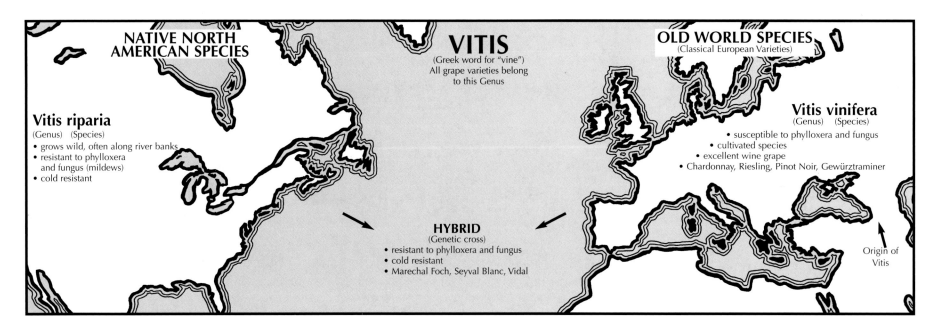

NATIVE NORTH AMERICAN SPECIES

VITIS
(Greek word for "vine")
All grape varieties belong to this Genus

OLD WORLD SPECIES
(Classical European Varieties)

Vitis riparia
(Genus) (Species)
• grows wild, often along river banks
• resistant to phylloxera and fungus (mildews)
• cold resistant

Vitis vinifera
(Genus) (Species)
• susceptible to phylloxera and fungus
• cultivated species
• excellent wine grape
• Chardonnay, Riesling, Pinot Noir, Gewürztraminer

HYBRID
(Genetic cross)
• resistant to phylloxera and fungus
• cold resistant
• Marechal Foch, Seyval Blanc, Vidal

Origin of Vitis

MONTH	APRIL	MAY	JUNE	JULY	AUGUST	SEPT.–OCT.	NOV.–FEB.
LIFE OF THE VINE — GRAPEVINE PHYSIOLOGY							BEFORE PRUNING / AFTER PRUNING

USE OF CARBO-HYDRATES							
PLANT	Budbreak	Grand Period of Growth		Growth Slows	Storage in Roots & Wood	Wood Maturity	∘Pruning
FRUIT		Flower Formation	Bloom - Set	Fruit - Bud Differentiation	*Veraison	Fruit Maturity Harvest	Icewine Harvest

GRAPE VARIETIES

White

CHARDONNAY
(Shar'-doe-nay)

AUXERROIS
(Oaks-air-wah')

RIESLING
(Reese-ling)

GEWÜRZTRAMINER
(German - Ge-vertz'-tram-mé-ner;)
(French - Gevoorts'-tram me-nair)

The reigning "King" of Burgundy is responsible for some of the most famous, and undoubtedly finest, dry white wines in the world. Prized for its stellar quality, Chardonnay is now widely planted throughout the wine regions of the world.

HARVEST – mid-season ripening: late-September to early October
SOILS – preference for clay-limestone soils
CLIMATE – performs best in cool climates
YIELDS – low: (40 - 60 hl/ha)*

An early ripening variety, commonly known as Petite Chardonnay, which produces light, refreshing white wine. Best known for its popularity in Alsace.

HARVEST – early ripening: mid-September
SOILS – deep, fertile soils, clay, clay/loam
CLIMATE – cool climates preferred
YIELDS – moderate: (60 – 80 hl/ha)

This variety is often said to be to Germany what the Chardonnay is to France. Like Chardonnay, Riesling is one of the "noble" varieties, and as such its popularity has led to plantings throughout the world. Riesling, by nature, carries a fairly high acidity, particularly in cool climates. This makes an excellent counterweight for varying degrees of residual sugar in the wines. This natural acid backbone allows Rieslings, whether made sweet or dry, to age gracefully and improve and develop over time.

HARVEST – late-ripening: mid- to late October
SOILS – preference for well drained, poor fertility.
CLIMATE – cool climates preferred
YIELDS – variable: (60 – 80 hl/ha average)

This is the grape whose highly aromatic and spicy wines have brought considerable fame and fortune to the vintners of Alsace. It tends to be fairly low in acidity, but at the same time highly flavourful.

HARVEST – mid-season ripening: late September
SOILS – deep, fertile loams with some clay
CLIMATE – cool climates preferred
YIELDS – low to moderate: (45 – 65 hl/ha)

Varietal: A varietal wine is any wine that is distinguished by and labelled according to the grape variety from which it was made. For example, Chardonnay wine is made from the Chardonnay grape. The VQA maintains strict regulations regarding the labelling of varietal wines.

* Hl/ha is the common measure of yield and refers to amount of juice measured in hundreds of litres (hecto-litres) per hectare of vineyard, for example, 40 hl/ha = 4000 litres from 1 hectare vineyard.

Red

CABERNET FRANC
(Cab'-air'nay Fronc)

PINOT NOIR
(Pee-no Nwahr)

CABERNET SAUVIGNON
(Cab'-air-nay So'-vin-yawn)

MERLOT
(Mair-lo)

Cabernet Franc is perhaps most famous for its contribution to the truly great wines of Saint-Emilion, Bordeaux. It is also the sole constituent of most of the finest red wines of the Loire Valley in France.

HARVEST – late-ripening: mid- to late October
SOILS – clays (can withstand some wetness)
CLIMATE – moderate, requires fairly long season to ripen fully
YIELDS – moderate: (55 – 65 hl/ha)

Responsible for all the great red wines of Burgundy and one of the main varieties in French Champagne, this old, traditional, yet temperamental grape has long been admired for its superlative quality. Pinot Noir produces wines of much more finesse in regions of moderate heat, and particularly in areas where the late-season nights tend to be quite cool. There is a very pronounced relationship between the yield of Pinot Noir and the quality of the fruit produced.

HARVEST – mid–season ripening: early October
SOILS – well drained, calcareous soils
CLIMATE – cool climates preferred
YIELDS – very low: (25 – 40 hl/ha)

The red grape of Bordeaux, and in particular, of the Medoc and Graves, Cabernet Sauvignon's popularity has taken it far from its native Bordeaux to the vineyards of both North and South America, Australia, New Zealand and South Africa. Due in part to the thick skins of the berries and the high pulp to pip ratio, the wines from this grape can be "massive," very deeply coloured and extremely tannic, particularly in warm climates. These characteristics give the wine a natural affinity for oak aging, and as a result are long-lived, sturdy and greatly improved with age.

HARVEST – late-ripening: mid- to late October
SOILS – less fertile, well drained
CLIMATE – warm, long growing season
YIELDS – low: (35 – 50 hl/ha)

The third variety of the classic Bordeaux trio of noble grapes, the Merlot currently occupies more hectares of Bordeaux vineyard than both Cabernets together. Although it is the sole constituent of such fine wines as the classified growths of Saint-Emilion and Pomerol, it is most often blended with the Cabernets to add a softening touch to the wine. Merlot wine is naturally supple and velvety smooth due to its soft tannins and relatively low acidity.

HARVEST – mid-season: early to mid- October
SOILS – clays
CLIMATE – moderate, not too wet during ripening
YIELDS – generous: (70 – 80 hl/ha with quality)

HARVESTING

CROSS-SECTION OF A RIESLING GRAPE

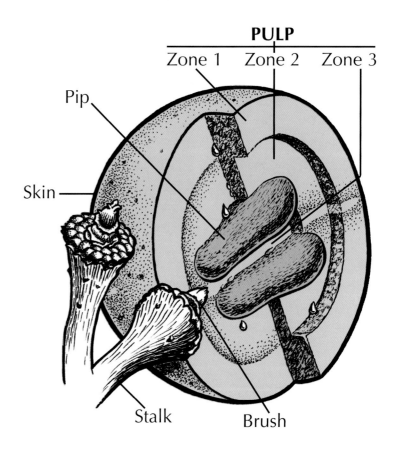

PULP

Zone 1   Zone 2   Zone 3

Pip

Skin

Stalk

Brush

Zone 2 releases its juice first. **Zone 1** is in contact with the skin and **Zone 3** with the pips, thus requiring gentle pressure for complete juice extraction.

When the grapes are harvested from the vineyard and delivered to the winery, they are inspected for maturity, ripeness (sugar content, acid and pH) and soundness to determine the beginning of the winemaking process.

The ripeness or sugar content of the grapes is ascertained by the winemaker's palate and is measured technically by the use of a refractometer (see illustration). The grape sugars are also monitored throughout the growing season in the vineyard by taking samples with the refractometer during the ripening season.

Brix = Degrees Brix (also known as Balling) is a measurement used by winemakers to define the sweetness (relative maturity) of grapes. Degrees Brix refer to the percentage of dissolved solids in the juice (almost all of which are sugars) and can be used by the winemaker to calculate the natural potential alcohol of the wine to be made as illustrated in the chart below. As a rule of thumb, the natural potential alcohol can be calculated by dividing Brix by two.

The Refractometer

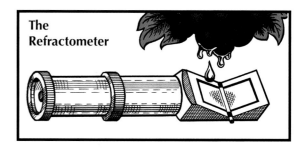

The reading in the refractometer (as illustrated right) indicates a **Brix** measurement of 21.5, which translates to 11.3% potential alcohol.

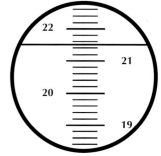

The chart below shows three systems for measuring the sugar content of grapes and their relationship to the potential alcohol of the resulting wine.

MEASUREMENTS OF SUGAR CONTENT

Specific Gravity	1.085	1.090	1.095	1.100	1.105
°Oechsle (Germany)	85	90	95	100	105
Baumé (France)	11.3	11.9	12.5	13.1	13.7
Brix (North America)	**20.4**	**21.5**	**22.5**	**23.7**	**24.8**
% Potential Alcohol	10.6	11.3	11.9	12.5	13.1

COOPERAGE The Art of Barrel Making

The use of oak in wine dates back over 2000 years.

Cooperage is the craft of making barrels and the craftsman is known as the cooper. The barrel making process for wine is an old and time-honoured one and is illustrated in its seven stages in the photographs on these pages.

The selection of wood used is as important to the cooper as the selection of grapes is to the winemaker. The winemaker can choose barrels made from many forests of oak. Many of the most prized are French (as illustrated below): Limousin,

Nevers, Troncais, Allier and Vosges. These different types of oak have varying degrees of porousness that range from "open grain" to "tight grain" (see page 38).

Winemakers also use American Oak which generally imparts more oak flavour, an almost "sweetish" taste used generally for heavier wines. European Oak contributes more extract and more tannin to wine and yet less flavour per unit of extract of phenolic compounds. Experienced tasters can often determine which oak was used in the aging of a particular wine.

THE OAK FORESTS OF FRANCE

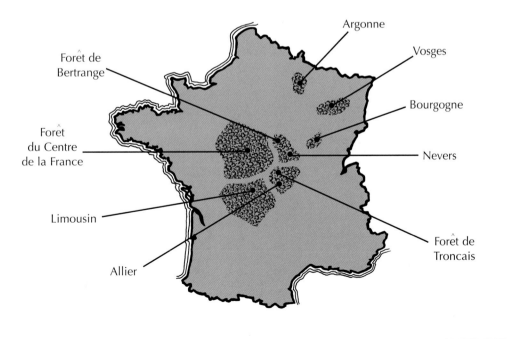

Argonne

Vosges

Forêt de Bertrange

Bourgogne

Forêt du Centre de la France

Nevers

Limousin

Forêt de Troncais

Allier

1. SPLITTING

2. DRYING

3. ASSEMBLING & SHAPING

4. FIRST FIRING

5. SECOND FIRING (toasting)

6. HEADS

7. FINISHING

HISTORY OF THE CORK

The use of natural cork as a closure for wine bottles is a centuries-old practice that continues today.

Cork is obtained from the layer just beneath the bark of the cork oak tree (*Quercus suber*) grown most extensively in Portugal (see photo top left), Spain and Algeria, and to a lesser extent in other Mediterranean countries.

The cork oak tree has a life span of 300-400 years, although they seldom grow to heights of more than twelve metres. The trees must be approximately fifty years of age before they produce cork of a quality suitable for wine stoppers.

Once a tree is ready for harvest, workers strip the bark using long-handled hatchets (see photo top right). This occurs during the months of June, July and August. Each individual tree may only be harvested once every eight to ten years.

Oblong sections of bark are carefully pried off the tree using the wedge-shaped handle of the hatchet. The inner layer of cork bark (the *peridium*) will continue to produce cork as long as it has not been bruised by the stripper's hatchet.

Slabs of stripped bark are then boiled and the tough, gritty outer layer is scraped off. The boiling dissolves tannic acid from the cork and softens the material so that the slabs can be straightened out, laid flat and packed into bundles.

The cork bottle closures are punched out of these slabs (see photo at right), sorted for quality, sterilized and packaged for shipment worldwide. At Inniskillin we use only the highest-grade quality corks for our wines.

DE-STEMMING/CRUSHING

Having been harvested, the grapes are delivered to the winery where they are immediately de-stemmed and crushed by means of a De-stemmer/Crusher. This process is quality driven since prolonged contact of the juice and the stems and leaves can impart undesirable bitterness to the resulting wine.

In the case of white winemaking from blue grapes, hand-harvested grapes are often pressed without being crushed. The pure crushed grapes (now called "must") are then pumped directly into the press.

Above: *Stainless steel auger.*

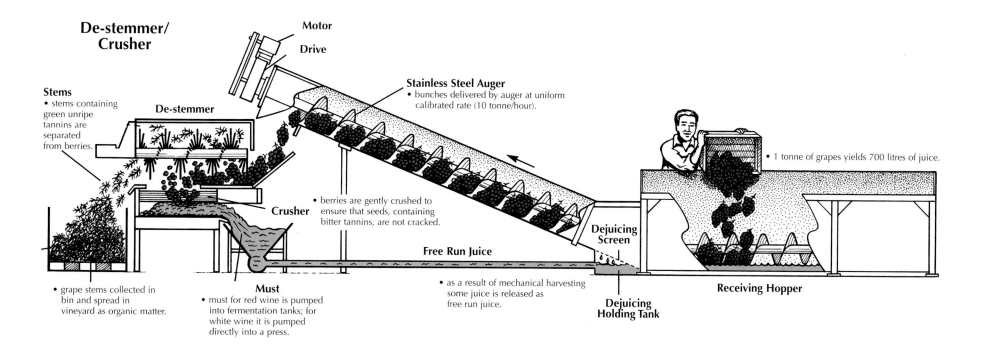

De-stemmer/Crusher

Motor

Drive

Stainless Steel Auger
• bunches delivered by auger at uniform calibrated rate (10 tonne/hour).

Stems
• stems containing green unripe tannins are separated from berries.

De-stemmer

• 1 tonne of grapes yields 700 litres of juice.

Crusher

• berries are gently crushed to ensure that seeds, containing bitter tannins, are not cracked.

Free Run Juice

Dejuicing Screen

• as a result of mechanical harvesting some juice is released as free run juice.

Receiving Hopper

• grape stems collected in bin and spread in vineyard as organic matter.

Must
• must for red wine is pumped into fermentation tanks; for white wine it is pumped directly into a press.

Dejuicing Holding Tank

PRESSING

The must goes directly into the grape press where the pure juice is then separated from the skins, pulp and seeds.

The Horizontal Pneumatic Press utilizes an inflatable bladder running the length of the press along a central shaft. When the press is loaded the bladder is in a collapsed state, tightly covering the shaft. As the must falls into the press the shaft slowly rotates, spreading it evenly inside the cage.

During this stage approximately 50 percent of the juice runs off through tiny perforations in the stainless steel cage of the press into a holding tank below. In principle, this press is identical to the traditional horizontal presses used throughout history. This pre-pressing run-off juice is referred to as "free run."

Once the press has been loaded to capacity, the cage is closed and then rotated for further de-juicing. The bladder can then be inflated inside the cage to press the grapes gently against the inside perforated wall of the cage.

The pressed de-juiced must, referred to at this stage as "pomace," is then unloaded from the press and can either be used for the distillation of brandy or be spread in the vineyard as organic mulch.

The Wine Press and the Information Revolution

Over 500 years ago, while watching wine being made, Johann Gutenberg noticed the impressions the wine press made in the must . He concluded that he could use the same principles to impress ink on paper – and the first printing press was born. Because of this monumental event, and thanks to the genius of Gutenberg and his love of wine, ideas and art have been reproduced and experienced by millions. So the next time you read a book, newspaper or magazine, make a toast to the art and power of wine.

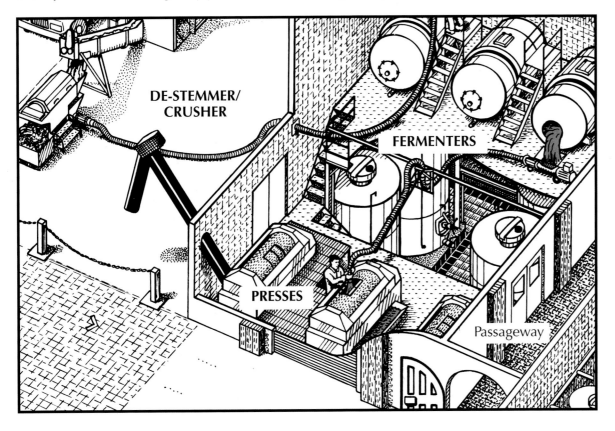

DE-STEMMER/CRUSHER

FERMENTERS

PRESSES

Passageway

Uninflated bladder over central shaft

perforated stainless steel press cage

must

free run wine

After pressing, white juice is pumped into tanks for clarification prior to fermentation. Red wine, already fermented, is pumped to tanks for fining.

CROSS-SECTION OF
HORIZONTAL PNEUMATIC PRESS

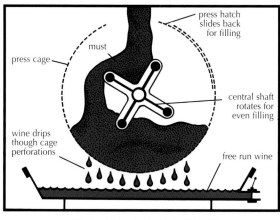

press hatch slides back for filling

must

press cage

central shaft rotates for even filling

wine drips though cage perforations

free run wine

FILLING THE PRESS

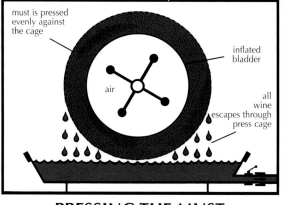

must is pressed evenly against the cage

inflated bladder

air

all wine escapes through press cage

PRESSING THE MUST

Right: *Free run white juice draining from press **prior** to fermentation.*

Far right: *Free run red wine as it drains from press **after** fermentation.*

FRESHLY PRESSED WHITE JUICE

FRESHLY PRESSED RED WINE

FERMENTATION

Colour & Tannin Extraction
(Red wine varieties and Chardonnay)

Since all grape juice is white, the pigmentation from the skins is extracted in order to produce red wine.

To achieve this in an **Upright Fermenter**, the must (skins, pulp, seeds and juice) is circulated every four hours.

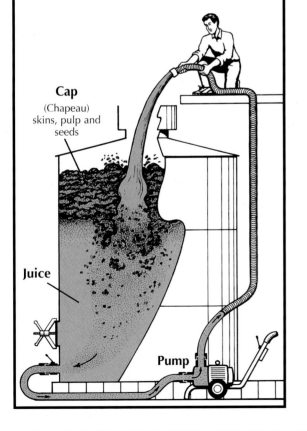

Cap
(Chapeau)
skins, pulp and seeds

Juice

Pump

Above: *Close up view of the **cap** (skins, pulp and seeds).*

Primary Alcoholic Fermentation

This is the process whereby yeast metabolizes the natural grape sugars, thus producing alcohol and carbon dioxide (CO_2) as the two main by-products. Technically this is how grape juice turns into wine.

The process of fermentation also generates a tremendous amount of heat (another by-product), and must therefore be controlled by the use of

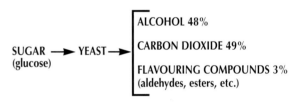

$$\text{SUGAR} \rightarrow \text{YEAST} \rightarrow \begin{cases} \text{ALCOHOL } 48\% \\ \text{CARBON DIOXIDE } 49\% \\ \text{FLAVOURING COMPOUNDS } 3\% \end{cases}$$
(glucose)   (aldehydes, esters, etc.)

Roto-Fermenter
As illustrated at right, the cap is mixed with the juice by the rotation of the "fins" inside the tank.

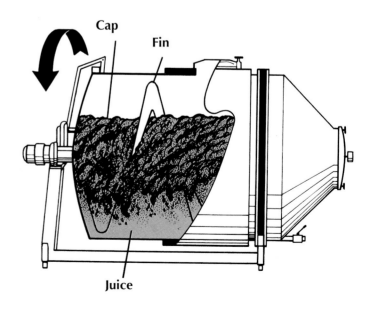

Cap

Fin

Juice

cooling jackets (bands of dimpled plates located on the outside of the tanks, circulating the cooling agent). The temperature of the fermentation is critical to the ultimate quality of the wine, especially white wine.

The rate of conversion of sugar to alcohol, being a natural process, is subject to many influences including temperature, yeast strain, yeast population, harvest variations and cellar conditions. As a result, fermentations can take as little as 24 hours to complete, or as much as one month or longer. A normal duration is approximately one week.

In a Roto-Fermenter, as illustrated on the opposite page, the "cap" (the name given to the skins, pulp and seeds) is mixed with the juice by the rotation of the fins inside the tank.

Malo-lactic Fermentation

Although not a true fermentation by technical definition, this is often referred to as a secondary fermentation. It is also referred to as "the flowering of the wine" because when it occurs in the spring, it coincides with the flowering of the vines or blossoming. Malo-lactic fermentation is an organic process performed by naturally occurring bacteria that feed on the wines' natural malic acid, converting it to the softer lactic acid. This process effectively reduces the overall natural acidity of the wine, and in so doing adds a certain character and complexity to the wine.

M-L, as it is commonly called, is known to enhance red wines and is therefore common practice in red wine vinification. However, it is only selectively encouraged in white wines.

Above: *Releasing of CO_2 through fermentation (air) locks.*

Chardonnay is the white wine variety most likely to benefit from M-L. Most other white wines of a more fruity character, and all naturally sweet wines, do not undergo an M-L fermentation.

Malic acid, derived from the Latin word *malum* or apple, indicates the sharp tartness of green apples. Lactic, derived from *lactis*, or milk, indicates the soft butteriness often used to describe Chardonnay. Malo-lactic fermentation is the process that transforms the one acid to the other and subsequently the one sensation to the other.

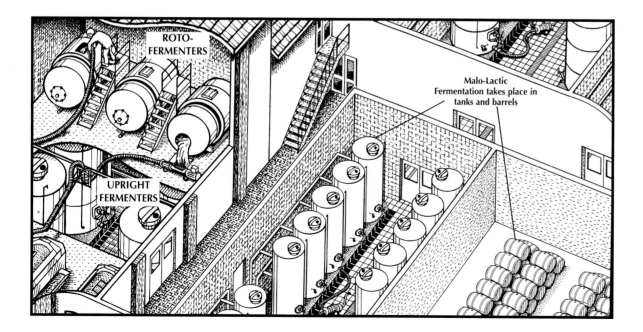

ROTO-FERMENTERS

UPRIGHT FERMENTERS

Malo-Lactic Fermentation takes place in tanks and barrels

RED WINES

After the red grapes are crushed and de-stemmed, the must is then pumped into a fermenting tank. It is inoculated with a pure strain yeast culture. The red must is fermented at temperatures between 25–30° C (much higher than the fermentation temperatures for white wine).

The colour of red wine is a result of the extraction of the colouring compounds from the grape skins, facilitated by the warmth created by the fermentation process. The carbon dioxide gas resulting from the fermentation causes the solid portion of the must to rise in the tank forming the cap. The extraction of colour takes place only in

the area of contact between the cap and the juice, which is also the zone of highest temperature. Therefore, in order to get the maximum extraction, the juice must somehow contact all of the skins. This can be achieved by several means.

Remontage is a method of pumping the juice from under the cap back over the top of it to soak

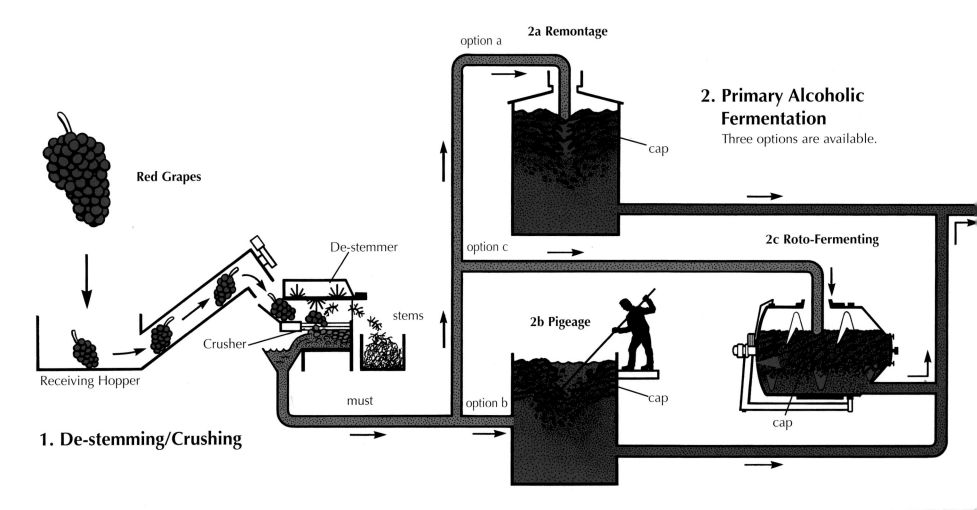

2a Remontage

option a

cap

2. Primary Alcoholic Fermentation

Three options are available.

Red Grapes

De-stemmer

stems

option c

2c Roto-Fermenting

Crusher

2b Pigeage

cap

cap

Receiving Hopper

must

option b

cap

1. De-stemming/Crushing

the drier skins on top. It mixes the cooler and warmer juice, and aerates the wine (to help perpetuate fermentation). Another option is the traditional Burgundian method of *pigeage*, in which the floating cap is physically pushed under the liquid and mixed in with it. Although the most demanding technique, this is also one of the most efficient in terms of extraction. In a Roto-Fermenter, which replicates *pigeage* with technology, the cap is mixed in with the juice by the rotation of the tank itself. Fins inside the tank fold the cap over the juice. This is an efficient technique, particularly adapted to accommodate larger volumes of must.

It is through the physical contact between the underlying juice and the cap that red wine acquires the colour, tannins and flavours that give it its character. Upon completion of the primary alcoholic fermentation, the fermented must is then pressed and sent to oak barrels or tanks where it undergoes malo-lactic fermentation.

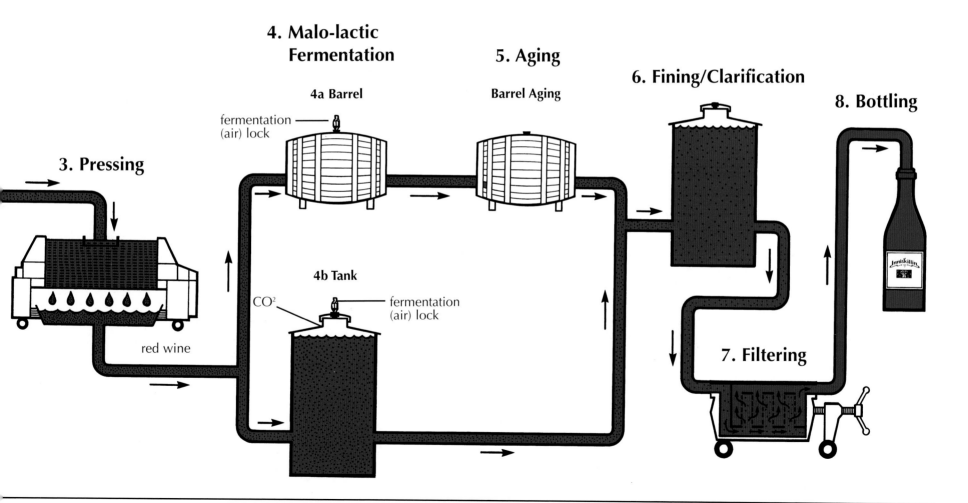

4. Malo-lactic Fermentation

4a Barrel

fermentation (air) lock

5. Aging

Barrel Aging

6. Fining/Clarification

8. Bottling

3. Pressing

red wine

4b Tank

CO_2

fermentation (air) lock

7. Filtering

WHITE WINES

All white wine grapes, having been analyzed for quality, are de-stemmed and crushed en route to the press. The must is then pressed in order to separate the juice from the skins, pulp and seeds.

The juice is then cooled to between 8 and 12° C on its way to the tank cellar for settling. The juice rests peacefully in a tank for a period of about 48 hours. During this time it is naturally clarified by the set-tling out of solids that are subsequently left behind in the tank by the "racking." Racking is the process of pumping the juice off the sediment to another tank. After racking, the clear juice is inoculated

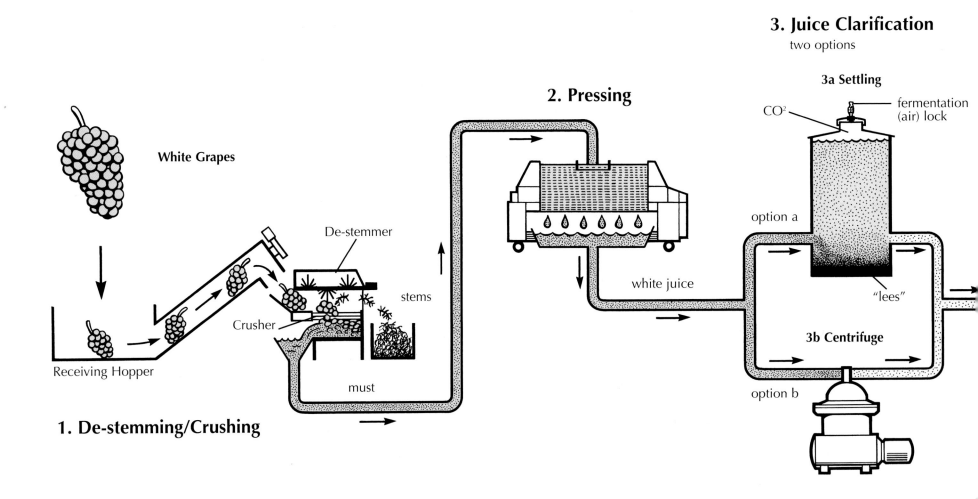

White Grapes

De-stemmer

stems

Crusher

must

Receiving Hopper

1. De-stemming/Crushing

2. Pressing

white juice

3. Juice Clarification
two options

3a Settling

CO_2

fermentation (air) lock

option a

"lees"

3b Centrifuge

option b

with a pure strain yeast culture which is responsible for the primary fermentation that changes the grape juice into wine. Following the inoculation, the juice may ferment in a stainless steel tank or in oak barrels, depending on the wine makers plan. Upon completion of the primary fermentation, a white wine is then racked into a stainless steel tank or into oak barrels for further aging.

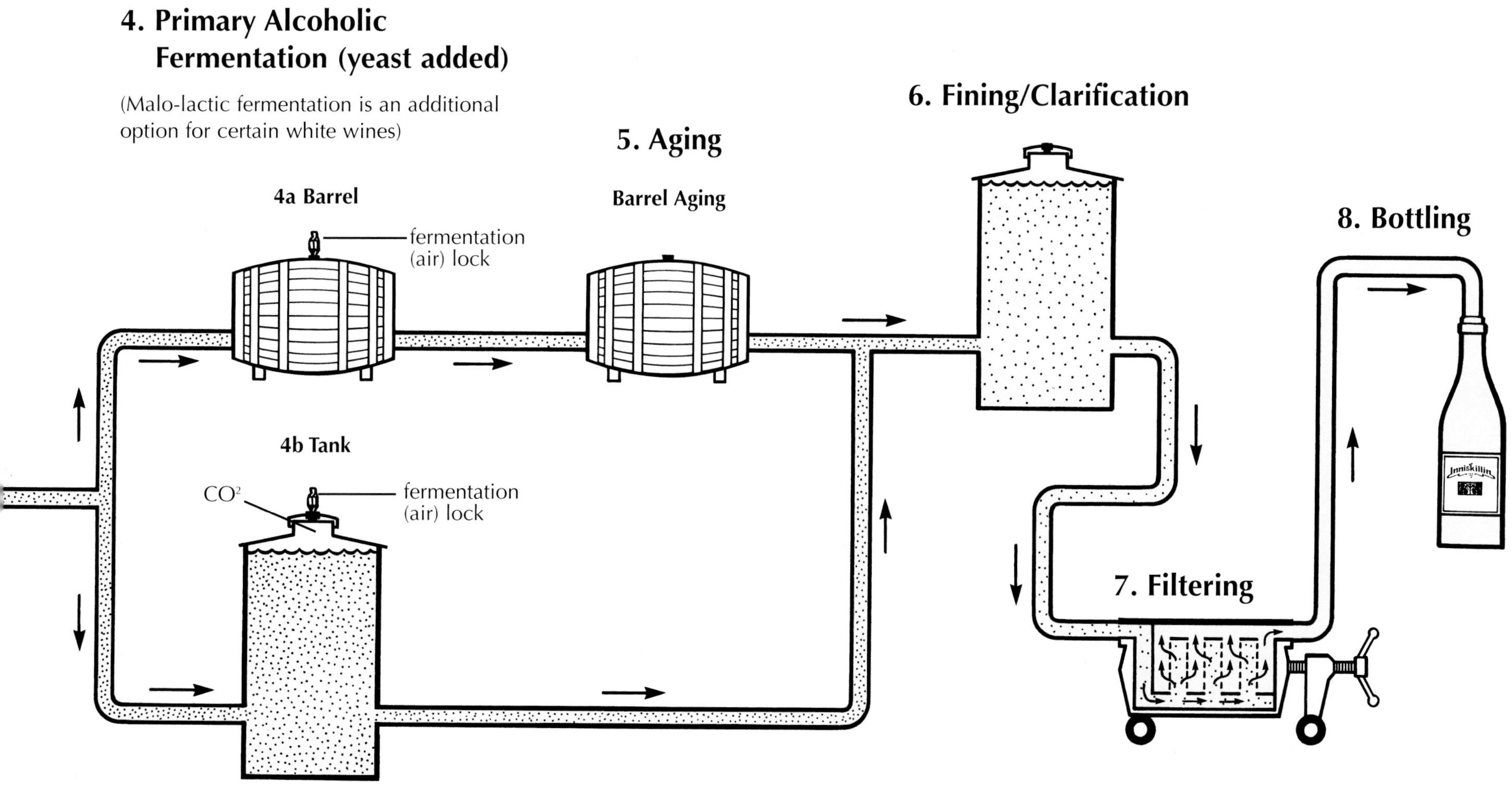

4. Primary Alcoholic Fermentation (yeast added)

(Malo-lactic fermentation is an additional option for certain white wines)

5. Aging

6. Fining/Clarification

8. Bottling

4a Barrel

fermentation (air) lock

Barrel Aging

4b Tank

CO_2

fermentation (air) lock

7. Filtering

TANK CELLAR

Settling/Clarification

Immediately following the pressing, the juice is cooled to 8–12° C in order to inhibit oxidation, yeast and enzyme activity, and to facilitate the settling out of solids in the juice. The removal of these solids is an important step prior to fermentation, as they can be a source of bitterness, off-odours and off-flavours in the resulting wine.

Fining

Fining is a dual-purpose procedure in which a fining agent is added to the wine in order to remove small suspended particles. This will serve to clarify the wine. It also stabilizes the wine by removing substances such as yeast cells and proteins that could cause cloudiness, spoilage or precipitation later on. When the fining agent is added, tiny particles cling to it and then settle to the bottom of the tank. The wine can then be either racked or filtered off the sediment, thus removing the particles and the fining agent at the same time. Commonly used fining agents include: gelatin, egg whites (see photo at right), isinglass (a natural fish-derived protein) and bentonite (a type of refined clay).

Filtration

Filtration, normally the final step in the vinification of a wine, is the process of pumping a wine through a filter medium under pressure. Basically a process of absorption, filtration serves to remove suspended particles, clarifying the wine. It also further removes possible contaminants such as residual yeast or bacteria, thereby stabilizing the wine as well. Barrel-aged wines do not necessarily require filtration.

Above: Egg whites being prepared for use as final fining agent.
Opposite page: Underground white wine cellar.

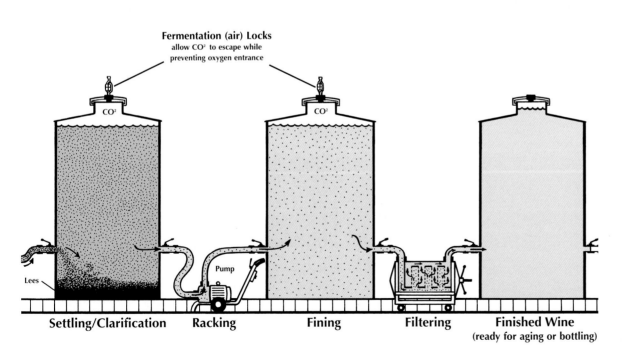

Fermentation (air) Locks
allow CO² to escape while preventing oxygen entrance

CO²   CO²

Pump

Lees

Settling/Clarification   Racking   Fining   Filtering   Finished Wine
(ready for aging or bottling)

BARREL AGING

BARREL AGING The Influence of Oak in Wine

The cost is high, approximately $700 per 225 litre barrel. Expensive? Yes! But many of the world's finest wines owe their share of character, complexity and quality to aging in small oak barrels. There are numerous variables when choosing a wine barrel. Each wine style requires a different oak flavour. The winemaker has the opportunity to choose the cooper, wood type, forest, grain, size of barrel and the toast. The grain may be "open" or "tight", as can be seen in the illustrations below. There are choices of barrel shape– Bordeaux (tall and narrow) and Burgundian (short and broad). There is also a choice between thinner staved "Chateau" and the thicker staved "Export" barrels.

The changes that occur during the wine's aging process are enormously complex. In barrel aging there are two aging functions. The first is extraction in which the tannins, vanilla, oak

GRAIN	FOREST	CHARACTERISTICS
OPEN	LIMOUSIN	Limousin wood perfumes and colours the wine rapidly with little finesse.
AVERAGE	BOURGOGNE NEVERS	Bourgogne and Nevers wood gives a vanilla flavour and balance to the wine.
TIGHT	ALLIER TRONCAIS VOSGES	The wood of Allier, Troncais and Vosges releases its perfumes slowly, with finesse.

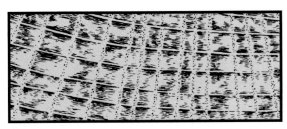

LIMOUSIN OAK - OPEN GRAIN

TRONCAIS OAK - TIGHT GRAIN

Main Level Storage

Underground Cellars

lactones and other phenolics are extracted from the wood. The second is oxidation in which tannins, acids and other components of the wine react to gradual exposure to oxygen through the grain of the wood.

The amount and type of aging that a wine should receive are both a function of the wine qualities such as colour or tannin, and the style of wine that is being produced.

For the first three years, barrels are used particularly for their extractives, as the total extractables offered up by the wood decrease dramatically after this time. In the fourth, fifth and sixth years a barrel is used primarily as a *barrique d'occasion* for the express purpose of slow oxidation (as the wood breathes) with a negligible absorption of extracts.

Tartrate crystals which appear on the barrel are naturally occurring crystals often referred to as "wine diamonds." When the grapes begin fermentation, they contain potassium from the soil where they grew and tartaric acid, a natural fruit acid present in ripe grapes. Through the increase in alcohol during fermentation, the potassium and the bitartrate of the tartaric acid are combined to form potassium bitartrate in solution form. Upon cooling, the solution changes to crystalline form and precipitates out of the wine. On occasion these crystals adhere to the barrel and may also occasionally occur in the bottle, most noticeably on the cork.

The barrel cellar on the main level is for the storage of red wines while the underground cellar, because it is cooler, is for the white wines.

Right: *Karl Kaiser (left) and Donald Ziraldo (right) sampling Pinot Noir Reserve.*

BOTTLING LINE

1. **Holding Tanks**
   Two stainless steel holding tanks for storing the wine to be bottled. The capacity of each tank is 12,000 litres or 16,000 750ml bottles.

2. **Final Filter**
   Wine is pumped from the bottling tanks through a filter (0.45 micron membrane filter) to the filler.

3. **Empty Glass**
   Glass arrives one day ahead of bottling.

4. **Bottle Rinser**
   Bottles are rinsed with filtered water to ensure complete sanitation and quality control.

5. **Bottle Filler**
   This filler is sterilized each day with steam. The fill level is carefully monitored to ensure compliance. The capacity of the line is 50 bottles per minute.

6. **Carbon Dioxide Injector**
   The head space in each bottle is injected with inert carbon dioxide gas to remove the normal air from the head space. This final blanket over the wine ensures that no oxygen remains, which otherwise might oxidize the wine.

7. **Natural Corker**
   The corks are inspected prior to being placed in the hopper. The corks are compressed from 24mm in diameter down to 15mm before entering the bottle. Once in the bottle the cork seals the neck by expanding to its original size.

8. **Capsule Dispenser**
   We do not use lead capsules on our bottles. Environmentally friendly capsules are rolled onto the bottle.

9. **Labeller**
   The labeller can apply front, back and shoulder labels at the same time.

10. **Shipping**
    Full pallets are then shipped to our environmentally controlled warehouse for storage.

BRAE BURN VINEYARD Station 18

Inniskillin's vineyard is called The Brae Burn Estate. Brae Burn is of Gaelic origin and translates literally as "Hill Stream," referring to the Niagara Escarpment and the Niagara River.

Brae Burn Estate, on which the winery is situated, is located on the Niagara Parkway just five minutes south of the historic town of Niagara-on-the-Lake and just twenty minutes north of Niagara Falls. The vineyard's soils consist of clay-loam with glacial and alluvial deposits, ideally suited for the growing of *Vitis vinifera* varieties, such as Pinot Noir. In addition, the winery is surrounded by vineyards dedicated to the production of Icewine.

Right: *View of Inniskillin from corner of Niagara Parkway and Line 3, with Niagara Escarpment in the background.*

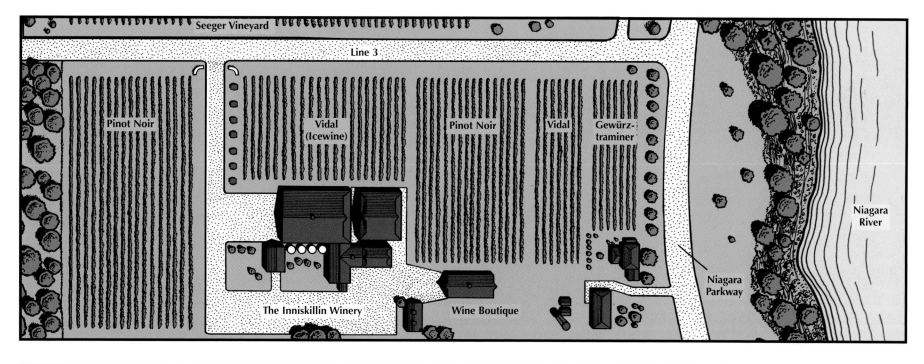

ICEWINE

Originally developed in the cool climate wine regions of Europe – Germany and Austria – the production of Icewine is ideally suited to Niagara's climatic conditions.

The grapes are left on the vine well into December and January. The ripe berries are dehydrated through the constant freezing and thawing during these winter conditions. This remarkable process concentrates the sugars, acids and extracts in the berries thereby intensifying the flavours and giving Icewine its immense complexity.

The entire vineyard is carefully covered with netting to protect the sweet ripe berries from ravaging birds. Some of the crop is lost to wind damage.

The grapes are painstakingly picked by hand in their naturally frozen state, ideally at temperatures of -10 to -13° C, sometimes forcing us to pick in the middle of the night. Yields are very low, often as little as 5–10 percent of a normal yield. The frozen grapes are pressed in the extreme cold. Much of the water in the juice remains frozen as ice crystals during the pressing and only a few drops of sweet concentrated juice are salvaged. The juice is then fermented very slowly for several months and stops naturally at approximately 10–12 percent alcohol.

Icewine tastes intensely sweet and flavourful in the initial mouth sensation. The balance is achieved by the acidity which creates a clean, dry finish to the taste. The nose is reminiscent of lychee nuts and the wine tastes of tropical fruits with overtones of peach nectar and mango.

HARVEST: December to January
HARVEST TEMPERATURES: -10° C to -13° C
PICKING: Hand harvested (exclusively), naturally frozen on the vine, normally throughout the night (coldest part of the day).
YIELD: Extremely low (approx. 5%–10% of a normal harvest)

Left: *Grand Prix d'Honneur Award from Vinexpo, Bordeaux, France, for 1989 Icewine.*
Above: *Naturally frozen grapes hanging on the vine prior to hand harvesting.*
Opposite page: *Pickers harvesting Icewine at 3:00 a.m., January 5, under the moonlight.*

FRANK LLOYD WRIGHT

When we originally acquired the Brae Burn Estate, one of the original buildings was an old barn with a long, simple pitched roof and unusual overhanging peaks. We discovered that this barn and two others on the Larkin Farm to the south were, in fact, "prairie barns," with ventilated overhangs pointed opposite to the prevailing winds to facilitate the drying of cereal grains and to protect them from blowing rain.

In March 1993, we installed the stained glass window (opposite page right) to commemorate the completion of the new barrel aging cellar. Inniskillin commissioned local Canadian artist Bonna Rouse to create this adapted reproduction from the originals designed by Frank Lloyd Wright for the Coonley Playhouse school building.

The commission was inspired by the fact that the barn that houses the Boutique and Art Gallery is very reminiscent of the Wright style. Darwin D. Martin, the president of the Larkin Company of Buffalo, was one of Frank Lloyd Wright's greatest patrons. Over the years, the Martin brothers were responsible for nine major Wright commissions in the Buffalo/Niagara Frontier area.

Frank Lloyd Wright revolutionized North American architecture. He rejected the classical designs borrowed from other worlds that so dominated the late nineteenth and early twentieth centuries. Instead he developed a form based on simplicity and the lessons of nature. He called it Organic Architecture.

Wright's bold marriage of natural form with modern creation is reflected in the Inniskillin philosophy of innovation inspired by tradition.

Right: *Front entrance of Wine Boutique in Brae Burn Barn.*
Opposite page left: *Front entrance to Barrel Aging Cellar.*
Opposite page right: *Stained glass reproduction of original Frank Lloyd Wright design.*

Station 20

It was his intent "to make the building belong to the ground", and at Inniskillin we have always designed the structures of our estate winery with this spirit in mind.

Not so much bound by tradition as inspired by it.

FOOD AND WINE

In our search for culinary excellence, we Canadians have discovered that distinctiveness and diversity exist here at home. Regional foods have joined with locally produced wines to form an identifiable, original Canadian culinary style, one that reflects the land, the people and the foods we produce.

Canadian chefs head into the country to stock their kitchens with locally grown fruits and vegetables. The Aboriginal people planted beans, squash and corn, foods now celebrated in Canadian cuisine. In Quebec, cheese varieties like Oka and Ermite Blue Cheese were developed over a century ago by local monks. Ontario's chefs are incorporating fiddleheads with maple syrup, and traditional game animals are being farmed, bringing venison and other delicacies back to the gourmet table. British Columbia's famed salmon forms the base of many brilliant new dishes. Recently, the Canadian Culinary Alliance was formed to promote the pairing of Canadian wines with locally produced foods. We are in the midst of an explosion of regional, seasonal cuisine.

Canadian wine, being cool climate wine, always retains a pleasant backbone of acidity, which clears the palate between bites. This makes Canadian wine an ideal partner to a wide variety of dishes.

In *The Food and Wine Adventure Series*, our resident chef, Isabela Kalabis, has married an array of Canadian foods to our line of varietal wines. The textures, aromas and flavours of the food mix with the body, aromas and flavours of the wines to create a truly unique Canadian gastronomic experience.

Let us not forget the simple pleasures of wine and food and their relevance to our daily lives.

INNISKILLIN OKANAGAN

Inniskillin Okanagan is a partnership between Inniskillin and the Inkameep Indian Band (Okanaquen Tribe) in the Okanagan Valley in British Columbia. The band has established 265 acres of vineyard and has dedicated itself to the growing of premium *Vitis vinifera* grapes on their ancestral lands.

The Inkameep chose to grow grapes on selected sites on the east side of the valley, which is part of the heritage of the region. We were impressed by the quality they have brought to viticulture in the region and we felt it was a wonderful opportunity for us to make wines that are unique to the region.

As Inniskillin Okanagan our first vintage was 1994. We used varieties such as Merlot, Pinot Noir, Chardonnay and Pinot Blanc. The labels were designed by a local artist. Great care was taken to ensure that the labels reflected the Native heritage. You will also notice in the photograph lower right, the famous McIntyre Bluff known as the Chief, which is famous in Indian legend.

The Okanagan Valley climatic region is much drier than Niagara and unique as a grape-growing region in western Canada. The valley is at the same latitude as the Rhine Valley in Germany and the Champagne region of France. The region stretches for 130 kilometres, from Lake Osoyoos (just north of the Canada/US border) to the northern tip of Okanagan Lake. The lakes moderate temperatures throughout the year. Intense sunlight and minimal rainfall allow grapes to ripen to their full maturity, while cool nights help them to retain high acidity. These climatic conditions, along with a unique soil structure, produce wines that are full-bodied and highly flavoured with good acidity.

Preceding page: *Smoked Short Hills trout from Niagara Escarpment (see map page 14) with local greens prepared by Chef Michael Olson.*

Top: *Petroglyph on wall inside of cave overlooking Inkameep Vineyard.*

Right: *Inkameep Vineyard with McIntyre Bluff in the background to the left.*

THE AUTHOR

Born in St. Catharines, Ontario, Donald J.P. Ziraldo is co-founder and President of Inniskillin Wines in Niagara-on-the-Lake, Ontario, Canada.

After receiving his Bachelor of Science Degree in Agriculture from the University of Guelph in 1971, Ziraldo joined forces with Karl J. Kaiser to found Inniskillin Wines in 1975.

Challenged by the need to compete on the world stage, Ziraldo pioneered the estate winery movement in Canada. As part of his ongoing efforts to promote quality wines produced in Canada, Ziraldo has been credited with founding the Vintners Quality Alliance (VQA), of which he is currently Chairman, an organization responsible for maintaining the highest standards in viticulture and winemaking. Ziraldo is also on the Board of Directors of the Canadian Culinary Alliance, which promotes awareness of Canada's indigenous cuisine and its marriage to Canadian wine.

Inniskillin's commitment to the Ontario wine industry has resulted in many gold medals from international wine competitions as proof of its success. In 1991 Inniskillin competed against 4100 wines from across the world in Vinexpo in Bordeaux, France, and captured the Citadel D'or Award (Grand Prix d'Honneur), the highest award, given for its 1989 Icewine.

While he continues to raise awareness of the quality of Ontario wines, Ziraldo is also driven by a desire to globalize. To this end he created an Import Division of Inniskillin to represent wines from around the world and established Inniskillin Napa Vineyards (Terra) in California's Napa Valley. In 1993 Inniskillin formed a partnership with the renowned Jaffelin of Burgundy, France, to produce wines from Pinot Noir and Chardonnay

grapes grown in Niagara, which are labelled under the name "ALLIĀNCE". More recently, in British Columbia's Okanagan Valley, Inniskillin is working with the Inkameep Indian Band (The Okanaquen Tribe) to create "Inniskillin Okanagan".

Ziraldo's leadership has earned him numerous awards from the business and wine communities. In 1993 he was appointed to the Order of Ontario, which honours service of the greatest distinction of singular excellence which benefits society in Ontario and elsewhere. Other awards include Marketer of the Year by the American Marketing Association and Canada's Grindley Medal (Agricultural Institute of Canada).

In 1994 he was also granted an honorary Doctor of Laws from St. Catharines' Brock University.

Ziraldo's passions lie in skiing and his Art Deco collection which graces his home on the Niagara River in Niagara-on-the-Lake.